Hydrogen Fuel Cells for Transportation

Contents

Preface
Introduction
Chapter 1: Introduction to Hydrogen as an Energy Source
Chapter 2: How Hydrogen Fuel Cells Work
Chapter 3: Hydrogen Fuel Cell Vehicles (HFCVs) Explained
Chapter 4: Applications of Hydrogen Fuel Cells in Transportation
Chapter 5: Production, Storage, and Distribution of Hydrogen
Chapter 6: Environmental and Economic Impact
Chapter 7: Challenges Facing Hydrogen Fuel Cell Adoption
Chapter 8: Future Trends in Hydrogen Fuel Cells for Transportation
Conclusion

Glossary

Preface

The global transportation sector is undergoing a profound transformation. Factors such as technological innovation, regulatory changes, and increased focus on environmental sustainability are driving this shift. Amid these changes, hydrogen fuel cells have emerged as a promising solution that could redefine the future of transportation. Hydrogen fuel cells offer a cleaner, scalable alternative to conventional fuel sources, addressing the dual challenges of reducing greenhouse gas emissions and meeting the growing energy needs of the transportation sector.

This book, *Hydrogen Fuel Cells for Transportation*, is part of the Gosships Learning Series and is aimed at providing a comprehensive understanding of hydrogen fuel cell technology for a wide audience—from beginners to those with an intermediate understanding of energy systems. We have structured the book to ensure that you not only grasp the fundamentals but also develop the knowledge necessary to apply these concepts in professional settings. With real-world applications, case studies, and key insights from industry experts, this book is a valuable resource for anyone seeking to navigate the complexities of hydrogen fuel cell technology.

This series is designed to provide foundational to intermediate knowledge, focusing on practical applications and real-world relevance. Every book in this series is paired with a certification test, ensuring that the knowledge gained is not only understood but can be directly applied in professional settings.

Our goal is to empower professionals to contribute to the adoption of this technology, which we believe will play a pivotal role in the transition to a more sustainable transportation system.

Introduction

Welcome to the *Gosships Learning Series*, designed for professionals eager to expand their knowledge and advance their careers in the maritime and energy sectors. This book, *Hydrogen Fuel Cells for Transportation*, has been carefully crafted by industry regulators and executives to ensure the content is both authoritative and aligned with today's industry standards. Whether you're new to the topic or looking to deepen your understanding, this resource will equip you with valuable insights to discuss hydrogen fuel cells confidently and expertly among your peers.

In this book, we'll explore the following key areas:

- **Hydrogen Production Methods**: Learn about electrolysis, steam methane reforming, and emerging techniques to generate hydrogen efficiently.

- **Hydrogen Storage and Transport**: Understand the challenges and solutions for safely storing and transporting hydrogen.

- **Applications of Hydrogen**: Discover how hydrogen is being used across multiple sectors, including transportation, industry, and energy production.

- **Environmental and Economic Considerations**: Explore the economic feasibility of hydrogen and its essential role in decarbonizing transportation and industries.

- **Hydrogen Safety**: Dive into modern safety protocols and technological advancements ensuring that hydrogen is handled securely.

Upon completing this book, you'll be ready to take an assessment designed to test your understanding of the material. After passing the assessment, you can obtain a *Certificate of Achievement* by visiting www.gosships.com and accessing the training platform. This certificate not only validates your expertise but also helps demonstrate your knowledge to peers and professionals in the industry.

Who is this book for?

This book is intended for:

- **Maritime and offshore personnel** looking to broaden their expertise.
- **Shoreside managers** seeking to enhance their understanding of emerging best practices.
- **Aspiring students** aiming to enter the industry with a solid foundation of hydrogen technologies.
- **Government and regulatory personnel** interested in staying informed about evolving industry standards.

By mastering the concepts presented in this book, you'll be well-equipped to face the challenges of modern operations, stay compliant with international regulations, and contribute to a safer, more efficient, and environmentally conscious work environment.

Thank you for selecting the *Gosships Learning Series* to support your continuous learning journey and professional growth.

Gosships Learning Series 2024/2025:

1. Hydrogen: The Fuel of the Future
2. Green Ammonia: The Next Big Thing in Shipping
3. Decarbonizing Shipping: Pathways to Zero Emissions
4. Battery Technology for Industrial Applications
5. Carbon Capture and Storage: Can It Save the Planet?
6. Biofuels 101: Turning Waste into Energy
7. Understanding LNG (Liquefied Natural Gas)
8. Methanol as a Marine Fuel
9. Offshore Wind Energy: The Future of Renewable Power
10. Tidal and Wave Energy: Harnessing the Ocean
11. Electrofuels: The Next Generation of Carbon-Neutral Fuels
12. Energy Storage Systems for Grid Reliability
13. Hydrogen Fuel Cells for Transportation
14. Solar Energy Innovations: Beyond Solar Panels
15. Smart Grids: The Backbone of Future Energy Systems
16. Ammonia-Hydrogen Blends: A Dual Fuel Solution?
17. Nuclear Power: Small Modular Reactors for a Low-Carbon Future
18. Hydropower: The Oldest Renewable Energy Source
19. Decentralized Energy Systems: Microgrids for Resilience
20. Energy Efficiency Technologies for Industry
21. Hydrogen Production from Seawater
22. Fuel Cells for Maritime Applications
23. Geothermal Energy: Unlocking Earth's Heat
24. Future of EV Charging Infrastructure

25. Synthetic Fuels: Bridging the Gap to Decarbonization
26. Cybersecurity for Maritime and Offshore Operations
27. AI and Automation in Shipping and Logistics
28. Digital Twins in Maritime: Revolutionizing Asset Management
29. Risk Management in Offshore and Maritime Operations
30. Compliance with IMO 2020 Regulations
31. Sustainable Ship Design: Reducing Environmental Impact
32. Marine Renewable Energy: Wave, Tidal, and Offshore Wind Integration
33. Ballast Water Management Systems
34. Blockchain Technology in Shipping: Improving Transparency & Efficiency
35. Effective Supply Chain Management for Energy Industries
36. Leadership in the Energy Transition
37. Effective Crisis Management in Maritime Operations
38. Shipyard Safety Management Systems
39. Port State Control (PSC) Inspection Readiness
40. Remote Vessel Operations and Autonomous Shipping
41. Optimizing Fleet Performance with Data Analytics
42. Maritime Environmental Regulations: Staying Ahead of Compliance
43. Advanced Maintenance Strategies: Condition Monitoring & Predictive Maintenance
44. Global LNG Market: Trends and Opportunities
45. Incident Investigation in Maritime Operations
46. International Maritime Law: Key Concepts and Applications
47. Emergency Preparedness and Response for Offshore Oil & Gas
48. Energy Transition Strategies for Oil and Gas Companies

49. Maritime Drones: Applications and Safety Considerations

50. Effective Project Management in Offshore Energy Projects

All Rights Reserved Disclaimer

The content in this book, including all text, graphics, images, logos, and designs, is the intellectual property of *Gosships LLC* and is protected under copyright law. No part of this publication may be reproduced, distributed, transmitted, or displayed without the prior written permission of the publisher, except for brief quotations in critical reviews or academic articles.

The information provided in this book is for educational purposes only, supplied "as is," without any warranties. The authors and publishers disclaim liability for any direct or indirect loss or damage arising from the use of material in this book.

For permissions or inquiries, please contact: admin@gosships.com.

© 2024 *Gosships LLC*. All rights reserved.

Chapter 1

Introduction to Hydrogen as an Energy Source

Hydrogen is the lightest and most abundant element in the universe, making it a highly promising energy source. However, hydrogen does not exist naturally in its pure form and must be extracted from compounds like water (H_2O) or natural gas. Historically, hydrogen has been used in industrial processes like oil refining and ammonia production, but its potential as a sustainable energy carrier has only recently gained widespread attention.

One of hydrogen's key advantages as an energy source is its high energy density. By weight, hydrogen contains three times more energy than gasoline, making it an ideal fuel for applications that require long-distance travel or heavy loads, such as freight transport and aviation. Additionally, hydrogen can be produced from a variety of sources, including renewable energy through a process called electrolysis, where water is split into hydrogen and oxygen using electricity.

Hydrogen is often referred to as a "clean" fuel because, when used in a fuel cell, it produces only water vapor as a byproduct, with zero harmful emissions. This makes hydrogen particularly attractive for industries like transportation, which are under increasing pressure to reduce their carbon footprints.

In this chapter, we will explore hydrogen's role as an energy carrier, focusing on its potential to revolutionize the transportation sector. We will also examine how hydrogen can be produced, stored, and utilized, and why it holds such promise as part of a future low-carbon economy.

Chapter 2

How Hydrogen Fuel Cells Work

Hydrogen fuel cells operate by converting the chemical energy in hydrogen into electrical energy through an electrochemical process. Unlike internal combustion engines, fuel cells do not burn hydrogen but instead use it in a reaction with oxygen to generate electricity, heat, and water. This process is highly efficient, clean, and scalable.

The most common type of fuel cell used in transportation is the Proton Exchange Membrane Fuel Cell (PEMFC). The PEMFC consists of several key components:

- **Anode:** Hydrogen is introduced at the anode, where it is split into protons and electrons. This reaction is facilitated by a catalyst, typically platinum.

- **Cathode:** Oxygen from the air is introduced at the cathode. Protons pass through an electrolyte membrane to reach the cathode, where they combine with electrons and oxygen to form water.

- **Electrolyte Membrane:** This membrane allows only protons to pass through, forcing the electrons to travel through an external circuit, generating electricity.

This reaction takes place in several steps:

1. Hydrogen enters the anode, where a catalyst causes the hydrogen molecules to separate into protons and electrons.

2. The protons pass through the membrane while the electrons are directed through an external circuit, creating an electric current.

3. At the cathode, the protons and electrons combine with oxygen to produce water, which is expelled as the only byproduct.

Hydrogen fuel cells are modular, meaning that they can be scaled up or down depending on the power requirements. This scalability makes fuel cells ideal for applications ranging from personal vehicles to heavy-duty trucks, trains, and even ships.

One of the key advantages of hydrogen fuel cells is their efficiency. While internal combustion engines are typically 25-30% efficient, hydrogen fuel cells can achieve efficiencies of up to 60%. This higher efficiency, combined with zero-emission output, positions hydrogen as a vital component of a sustainable transportation future.

Chapter 3
Hydrogen Fuel Cell Vehicles (HFCVs) Explained

Hydrogen Fuel Cell Vehicles (HFCVs) represent a significant leap forward in clean transportation. These vehicles use hydrogen stored in high-pressure tanks to generate electricity on board, which powers an electric motor and other vehicle systems. Unlike battery-electric vehicles (BEVs), which rely on stored electricity, HFCVs continuously generate electricity as long as they have hydrogen fuel.

An HFCV comprises the following key systems:

- **Hydrogen Storage Tank:** Hydrogen gas is stored under high pressure, typically at 700 bar.

- **Fuel Cell Stack:** This is the heart of the vehicle, where hydrogen is converted into electricity.

- **Electric Motor:** The motor drives the wheels, using electricity generated by the fuel cell.

- **Battery:** A small battery is used to store excess energy and provide additional power when needed, especially during acceleration.

HFCVs offer several benefits over BEVs, including:

- **Longer Range:** HFCVs typically offer a range of 300-400 miles, making them more suitable for long-distance travel compared to most BEVs.

- **Faster Refueling:** Hydrogen refueling takes about 3-5 minutes, similar to filling a gasoline tank, whereas BEVs can take anywhere from 30 minutes to several hours to charge.

- **Lower Weight for Heavy-Duty Vehicles:** Because hydrogen has a higher energy density by weight than batteries, HFCVs are more suited to heavy-duty applications such as buses and trucks.

As of today, there are several HFCVs available on the market, including the Toyota Mirai, Hyundai Nexo, and Honda Clarity Fuel Cell. These vehicles are primarily available in regions with established hydrogen refueling infrastructure, such as California, Japan, and parts of Europe.

The growing interest in HFCVs highlights the potential for hydrogen to complement other clean energy solutions, offering a flexible, high-performance alternative to battery-electric vehicles.

Chapter 4

Applications of Hydrogen Fuel Cells in Transportation

Hydrogen fuel cells are being increasingly recognized for their versatility in a wide range of transportation applications. While much attention has been given to hydrogen-powered cars, the technology has much broader potential.

- **Passenger Cars and Light-Duty Vehicles:** Hydrogen fuel cell cars provide a practical alternative to battery-electric vehicles, especially for drivers who need longer ranges and faster refueling times.

- **Buses and Trucks:** Hydrogen is well-suited for heavy-duty vehicles like buses and long-haul trucks. In cities across Europe, Asia, and North America, hydrogen buses are being deployed as part of efforts to reduce air pollution from diesel engines. Long-haul trucks powered by hydrogen are particularly promising because they overcome some of the limitations of battery-electric trucks, such as weight and long recharging times.

- **Maritime Transport:** The shipping industry is one of the largest contributors to global greenhouse gas emissions. Hydrogen fuel cells offer a pathway to reducing emissions from ships, ferries, and even submarines. As regulations tighten and consumers demand greener shipping practices, hydrogen-powered vessels are expected to play a major role in decarbonizing the maritime sector.

- **Aviation and Aerospace:** Hydrogen-powered aircraft are still in development, but the technology has the potential to transform the aviation industry. Short-haul regional flights powered by hydrogen fuel cells could offer a cleaner alternative to conventional jet fuel, reducing emissions and noise pollution.

- **Railways:** Hydrogen-powered trains, such as the Alstom Coradia iLint, are already operational in several countries. These trains offer a zero-emission alternative to diesel-powered trains, which are still widely used on non-electrified rail lines.

As hydrogen infrastructure expands, we can expect fuel cells to be deployed across even more transportation modes, helping to create a more sustainable global transport system.

Chapter 5

Production, Storage, and Distribution of Hydrogen

For hydrogen fuel cells to be widely adopted in transportation, the production, storage, and distribution of hydrogen must be economically and environmentally sustainable. Currently, there are three primary methods of producing hydrogen:

1. **Electrolysis:** Water is split into hydrogen and oxygen using electricity. If the electricity is generated from renewable sources, the resulting hydrogen is known as "green hydrogen." This is the most sustainable method but currently accounts for only a small percentage of global hydrogen production due to the high costs associated with renewable energy and electrolysis technology.

2. **Steam Methane Reforming (SMR):** This is the most common method of hydrogen production today, accounting for about 95% of hydrogen produced globally. In SMR, natural gas (methane) reacts with steam to produce hydrogen and carbon dioxide. While this method is cost-effective, it also generates significant CO_2 emissions, making it less environmentally friendly unless combined with carbon capture technologies.

3. **Thermochemical Water Splitting:** This method uses heat from sources such as solar energy or nuclear reactors to split water into hydrogen and oxygen. While promising, this technology is still in the experimental stages and has yet to be commercialized at scale.

Storage and distribution are equally challenging. Hydrogen can be stored as a gas under high pressure or as a liquid at cryogenic temperatures. Both methods require specialized infrastructure and equipment, which adds to the cost. For hydrogen to become a mainstream energy carrier, significant investments will be required to build the necessary infrastructure for its production, storage, and distribution.

Hydrogen can be distributed via pipelines or delivered by tanker trucks. In regions where hydrogen infrastructure is still developing, hydrogen is often transported in compressed gas cylinders or as a liquid. However, building a widespread hydrogen distribution network will be essential for the widespread adoption of hydrogen fuel cells in transportation.

Chapter 6

Environmental and Economic Impact

One of the primary motivations behind the push for hydrogen fuel cells is their potential to reduce greenhouse gas emissions. When powered by green hydrogen, fuel cells produce only water vapor, making them a zero-emission technology. This is especially important in the transportation sector, which is one of the largest contributors to global CO_2 emissions.

- **Environmental Impact:** The transportation sector accounts for nearly a quarter of global CO_2 emissions, making it a critical target for decarbonization efforts. Hydrogen fuel cells offer a pathway to significantly reduce emissions from cars, buses, trucks, ships, and planes. Hydrogen also has the potential to reduce reliance on fossil fuels, which are finite and contribute to global climate change.

The environmental benefits of hydrogen fuel cells are even more significant when green hydrogen is used. Green hydrogen is produced using renewable energy sources such as wind, solar, or hydropower. This makes hydrogen fuel cells a key component of a broader clean energy system, complementing renewable energy by providing a means of storing and using excess energy generated during periods of high renewable output.

- **Economic Impact:** While hydrogen fuel cells offer long-term economic benefits, particularly in terms of reduced fuel and maintenance costs, the initial investment required to build hydrogen infrastructure is high. Hydrogen production, storage, and distribution systems must be scaled up to support widespread adoption, and fuel cell vehicles (FCEVs) remain more expensive than their battery-electric (BEV) or internal combustion engine (ICE) counterparts.

However, governments worldwide are increasingly recognizing the potential of hydrogen and are investing in the development of hydrogen infrastructure. Subsidies and tax incentives are being introduced to make hydrogen vehicles more affordable and to encourage the development of hydrogen refueling stations. As these investments continue, the costs of hydrogen fuel cell technology are expected to decrease, making it a viable option for a broader range of applications.

Chapter 7

Challenges Facing Hydrogen Fuel Cell Adoption

While hydrogen fuel cells offer immense potential, several challenges must be overcome for them to achieve widespread adoption. These challenges include high production costs, a lack of infrastructure, and public awareness issues.

- **Cost:** The high cost of producing hydrogen fuel cells is one of the biggest barriers to adoption. Fuel cells require expensive materials, such as platinum, to function efficiently. While advances in technology are helping to reduce costs, fuel cell vehicles remain more expensive than conventional gasoline-powered cars and battery-electric vehicles.

- **Infrastructure:** Another major challenge is the lack of hydrogen refueling infrastructure. While electric vehicle (EV) charging stations are becoming more common, hydrogen refueling stations are still relatively scarce, especially outside of regions like California, Japan, and Europe. For hydrogen fuel cells to become a viable alternative to internal combustion engines or battery-electric vehicles, a global network of hydrogen refueling stations must be established.

- **Public Awareness and Acceptance:** Hydrogen fuel cell technology is still relatively unknown to most consumers. While battery-electric vehicles are becoming more mainstream, public knowledge of hydrogen's potential as a clean energy solution remains limited. Overcoming this challenge will require education campaigns, demonstration projects, and increased visibility of hydrogen-powered vehicles on the road.

- **Hydrogen Production:** Currently, most hydrogen is produced from natural gas through steam methane reforming, which emits significant amounts of CO_2. For hydrogen fuel cells to truly contribute to a low-carbon future, a shift toward green hydrogen production is necessary. This will require large-scale investments in renewable energy infrastructure and improvements in electrolysis technology.

- **Storage and Transportation:** Hydrogen is a highly volatile gas, and its storage and transportation present unique challenges. It must be stored under high pressure or at extremely low temperatures when liquefied, both of which require specialized infrastructure. Additionally, transporting hydrogen across long distances involves significant energy input, which can offset some of the environmental benefits.

- **Regulatory Support:** Governments play a crucial role in supporting hydrogen fuel cells through policies and incentives. Regulatory frameworks must be established to support hydrogen infrastructure development, and carbon pricing mechanisms should be introduced to encourage the adoption of clean technologies. Without consistent long-term policy support, the adoption of hydrogen fuel cells may be slow.

Chapter 8

Future Trends in Hydrogen Fuel Cells for Transportation

The future of hydrogen fuel cells looks promising, with several trends indicating that hydrogen may play a key role in the future of transportation.

1. **Technological Advancements:** Research and development efforts are focused on improving the efficiency and durability of fuel cells while reducing costs. One area of research is the development of new materials for catalysts, which could reduce the need for expensive platinum. Improvements in electrolyzer technology are also expected to make green hydrogen production more cost-effective.

2. **Policy and Government Support:** Governments around the world are recognizing the potential of hydrogen as a clean energy solution. Many countries, including Japan, Germany, and South Korea, have introduced hydrogen strategies that include investments in hydrogen infrastructure, research and development, and subsidies for hydrogen fuel cell vehicles.

3. **Infrastructure Expansion:** As more hydrogen refueling stations are built, particularly in regions like Japan, Europe, and the U.S., refueling challenges will diminish. The expansion of hydrogen infrastructure is critical for making hydrogen vehicles more practical and accessible to consumers.

4. **Integration with Renewable Energy:** One of the most promising trends is the integration of hydrogen production with renewable energy sources. Hydrogen production via electrolysis, powered by wind or solar energy, offers a truly sustainable fuel option. By producing hydrogen during periods of excess renewable energy production, hydrogen fuel cells can help balance energy supply and demand in a green economy.

Hydrogen is expected to complement other clean energy technologies, such as battery-electric vehicles and renewable energy storage, creating a diverse and flexible energy ecosystem that can meet the world's growing energy needs.

Conclusion

Hydrogen fuel cells represent one of the most exciting and promising technologies for transforming the global transportation sector. As the world shifts towards cleaner, more sustainable energy sources, hydrogen stands out as a key player in reducing emissions, promoting energy independence, and enabling the transition to a low-carbon economy.

Despite the challenges that remain, such as high production costs, infrastructure limitations, and public awareness issues, the potential of hydrogen fuel cells is undeniable. Governments, businesses, and research institutions are increasingly investing in the development of hydrogen technologies, and progress is being made in areas like green hydrogen production, fuel cell efficiency, and infrastructure expansion.

The environmental benefits of hydrogen fuel cells are clear. They produce zero emissions at the point of use, making them an ideal solution for reducing air pollution and combating climate change. Hydrogen can also be produced from renewable energy sources, offering a sustainable alternative to fossil fuels. In the long term, hydrogen fuel cells could play a crucial role in decarbonizing not only the transportation sector but also industries like shipping, aviation, and rail.

Moreover, the economic benefits of hydrogen fuel cells should not be overlooked. While the initial investment in hydrogen infrastructure and technology is high, hydrogen fuel cells offer long-term cost savings through reduced fuel consumption and maintenance costs. As governments continue to introduce incentives and support for hydrogen technologies, the cost of hydrogen fuel cells is expected to decrease, making them more accessible to consumers and businesses alike.

In conclusion, hydrogen fuel cells have the potential to revolutionize the transportation industry and play a central role in the global transition to a clean energy future. By continuing to invest in infrastructure, research, and public education, hydrogen fuel cells can help create a cleaner, more sustainable world. The road ahead may be challenging, but the rewards—both environmental and economic—are worth the effort. As you finish this book, we hope you are inspired to become part of this transformative journey towards a greener future powered by hydrogen.

Glossary - Hydrogen Fuel Cells for Transportation

1. **Anode** – The positively charged electrode where oxidation occurs in a hydrogen fuel cell.
2. **Balance of Plant (BoP)** – The auxiliary components that support the fuel cell system, including pumps, sensors, and compressors.
3. **Battery Electric Vehicle (BEV)** – A vehicle powered by an electric battery, distinct from hydrogen fuel cell vehicles.
4. **Carbon Dioxide (CO_2)** – A greenhouse gas produced by burning fossil fuels, which hydrogen fuel cells aim to reduce.
5. **Catalyst** – A substance that increases the rate of a chemical reaction without undergoing any permanent change, used in fuel cells to facilitate hydrogen oxidation.
6. **Compressed Hydrogen (CH_2)** – Hydrogen stored under high pressure to increase its energy density.
7. **Diffusion Layer** – A component of the fuel cell that helps evenly distribute gas across the electrode surface.
8. **Direct Methanol Fuel Cell (DMFC)** – A type of fuel cell that uses methanol as the fuel, rather than hydrogen.
9. **Electrochemical Reaction** – A reaction in which electrons are transferred between chemicals, key to fuel cell operation.
10. **Electrolysis** – A process of using electricity to split water into hydrogen and oxygen.
11. **Electrolyzer** – A device that performs electrolysis to produce hydrogen from water.
12. **Energy Density** – The amount of energy stored per unit volume or mass, important for fuel cell efficiency.
13. **Fuel Cell Electric Vehicle (FCEV)** – A vehicle powered by hydrogen fuel cells, producing electricity onboard.
14. **Fuel Cell Stack** – Multiple fuel cells connected together to generate a higher voltage and power output.
15. **Green Hydrogen** – Hydrogen produced using renewable energy sources, such as wind or solar power.
16. **Hydrogen (H_2)** – The most abundant element in the universe, used as a clean fuel in hydrogen fuel cells.
17. **Hydrogen Infrastructure** – The network of refueling stations, pipelines, and storage facilities supporting hydrogen-powered vehicles.
18. **Hydrogen Production** – The process of generating hydrogen, through methods like electrolysis or steam methane reforming.
19. **Hydrogen Refueling Station (HRS)** – A station where hydrogen vehicles can refill their hydrogen tanks.
20. **Hydrogen Storage** – Methods and technologies used to safely store hydrogen, either as a gas, liquid, or in solid-state form.
21. **Ion Exchange Membrane** – A membrane that allows selective ion transfer in a fuel cell, crucial for separating hydrogen from oxygen.

22. **Kilowatt (kW)** – A unit of power, commonly used to measure the output of hydrogen fuel cells.
23. **Kilowatt-Hour (kWh)** – A measure of energy consumption equivalent to using one kilowatt of power for one hour.
24. **Liquefied Hydrogen (LH2)** – Hydrogen that has been cooled to a liquid state, allowing more efficient storage and transport.
25. **Membrane Electrode Assembly (MEA)** – The core component of a fuel cell where the electrochemical reaction occurs.
26. **Net Zero Emissions** – The balance of emitted and absorbed greenhouse gases, a target for hydrogen fuel cells to achieve.
27. **Oxidation** – A chemical reaction involving the loss of electrons, happening at the anode in a fuel cell.
28. **Oxygen (O2)** – Used in fuel cells as the oxidant at the cathode, reacting with hydrogen to produce water.
29. **Passenger Fuel Cell Vehicle (PFCV)** – A fuel cell-powered vehicle designed for personal transportation.
30. **Permeability** – The ability of a material to allow fluids or gases to pass through, important for fuel cell membranes.
31. **Platinum (Pt)** – A common catalyst material used in hydrogen fuel cells due to its effectiveness in facilitating reactions.
32. **Polyelectrolyte** – A polymer with electrically charged groups, used in proton exchange membranes.
33. **Proton Exchange Membrane (PEM)** – A key component in PEM fuel cells, allowing protons to move while blocking gases.
34. **Proton Exchange Membrane Fuel Cell (PEMFC)** – A type of hydrogen fuel cell that operates at low temperatures, commonly used in transportation.
35. **Reformer** – A device used to extract hydrogen from hydrocarbons, such as natural gas.
36. **Renewable Energy** – Energy from sources that are replenished naturally, like wind or solar power, often used for hydrogen production.
37. **Stack** – The assembly of individual fuel cells that together generate the power required for applications like vehicles.
38. **Steam Methane Reforming (SMR)** – A method of producing hydrogen by reacting methane with steam.
39. **Storage Tank** – A vessel used to store hydrogen, either in gaseous or liquid form.
40. **Sustainable Transportation** – Transport methods that minimize environmental impact, including the use of hydrogen fuel cells.
41. **Thermal Efficiency** – A measure of how efficiently energy is converted to work, important in evaluating fuel cell performance.
42. **Transport Layer** – The layer in a fuel cell stack that helps manage the movement of water and gases.
43. **Vehicle-to-Grid (V2G)** – A technology allowing fuel cell vehicles to return electricity to the grid when needed.
44. **Voltage** – The potential difference in an electrical circuit, which drives

the flow of current in a fuel cell.
45. **Water Electrolysis** – A process of splitting water into hydrogen and oxygen using electrical energy.
46. **Water Vapor** – The only emission produced by hydrogen fuel cells during operation.
47. **Watt (W)** – A unit of power, used to measure the output of fuel cells.
48. **Zero Emission Vehicle (ZEV)** – A vehicle that produces no tailpipe emissions, such as a hydrogen fuel cell vehicle.
49. **Zero-Carbon Fuel** – Fuel that emits no carbon during its production and consumption, such as hydrogen.
50. **Zinc-Air Battery (ZAB)** – A battery technology that could complement hydrogen fuel cells for energy storage.

www.ingramcontent.com/pod-product-compliance
Lightning Source LLC
Chambersburg PA
CBHW030109230526
45471CB00003B/1337